nothing to hear-say

The Popstars band was chosen. Five people, the youngest of whom was 19 and the eldest 24, had suddenly become among the most instantly recognisable faces in Britain — and that was before they had brought out a single or even come up with a name for their new band.

So who exactly were they?

nothing but hear'say

Fergus Kelly

SCHOLASTIC

Scholastic Children's Books
Commonwealth House, 1-19 New Oxford Street
London WC1A 1NU
a division of Scholastic Ltd
London ~ New York ~ Toronto ~ Sydney ~ Auckland
Mexico City ~ New Delhi ~ Hong Kong

First published in the UK by Scholastic Ltd, 2001

Text copyright © Fergus Kelly, 2001

ISBN 0 439 98091 7

All rights reserved

2 4 6 8 10 9 7 5 3 1

Printed by Cox & Wyman Ltd, Reading, Berks

The publishers would like to thank the following sources for their kind permission
to reproduce the pictures in this book:

Front Cover: PA Photos / William Conran; Back Cover: PA Photos / Peter Jordan
Colour insert: **Pg 1**: Pic ©London Features International; **Pg 2**: Pic ©London Features International; **Pg 3**: Pic ©London Features International; **Pg 4**: Pic ©London Features International (top); PA Photos / William Conran (bottom); **Pg 5**: PA Photos / Peter Jordan; **Pg 6**: Pic ©London Features International; **Pg 7**: Pic ©London Features International; **Pg 8**: Pic ©London Features International

This book is sold subject to the condition that it shall not, by way of trade or otherwise
be lent, resold, hired out, or otherwise circulated without the publisher's prior consent in
any form of binding or cover other than that in which it is published and without a similar
condition, including this condition, being imposed on a subsequent purchaser.

This book is not authorised or endorsed by Hear'say or their management or by the
creators of the *Popstars* television series.

For Nikki and Daniel

Contents

chapter one
By Royal Appointment   9

chapter two
Nigel, Pick Me!   11

chapter three
Walking The Green Mile   25

chapter four
Welcome To The Band   37

chapter five
Kym 47

chapter six
Danny 57

chapter seven
Myleene 63

chapter eight
Noel 69

chapter nine
Suzanne 75

chapter ten
From Popstars To Hear'say 81

chapter eleven
Pure And Simple 93

chapter twelve
And The Future ...? 101

chapter one
By Royal Appointment

They were on the same bill as international stars such as Mel B of The Spice Girls, Lionel Richie and Dame Shirley Bassey. The venue was London's Royal Albert Hall. And the guest of honour was the Duke of Edinburgh.

Yet the five people about to perform at this gala night to mark the Duke's 80th birthday had, only a year previously, been a waiter, a backing singer, an office cleaner, a single mum-of-two, and a member of an Abba tribute band. They had also been unknown to each other.

In the intervening months, the five of them had become closer to one another than anyone else outside their immediate families, and, thanks to a television series which was watched by millions of viewers, they had been transformed into some of the best known and most talked about faces in the country. Then they had been behind the year's biggest selling single. Their performance, during which they sang three songs in front of the Duke, was the most eagerly awaited part of the show.

As a result, it was they who were pictured with Prince Philip in all the following morning's national newspapers, rather than the other leading names who had attended the evening.

Their appearance put a royal seal on an extraordinary rise to the top, which had begun nine months earlier, in a series of auditions held all over the country.

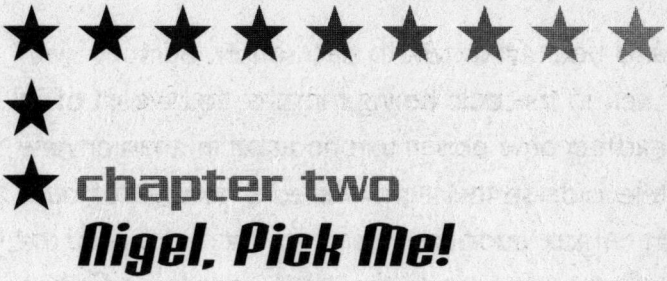

chapter two
Nigel, Pick Me!

It was over the Christmas and New Year holidays of 2000 that the television commercials and advertisements began to appear. Billboards up and down the country bore the words: 'Nigel, pick me!' But who was Nigel, and what was he picking?

The answer to that lay in an advert that was placed in *The Stage* newspaper on August 10 of that year. Headed 'WANTED: POPSTARS', it asked: 'Have you got what it takes to be a star?

Are you aged 18-24 and simply bursting with talent? This could be your chance to be part of an exciting new pop group and star in a major new television series.' It then listed a number of cities in which auditions were to be held and the telephone numbers to call for those interested. Only six years previously, a similar advert in the same newspaper had led ultimately to the formation of The Spice Girls.

    The advert had been placed by London Weekend Television, and the man behind it was one of the company's most experienced executives, Nigel Lythgoe. In a long and varied career, he'd gone from being a dancer in his youth, to arranging dance routines on *The Muppet Show* for the likes of Miss Piggy. He'd then moved into producing shows for such big names as Morecambe and Wise, the most popular comedy duo in Britain between the 1960s and the 1980s. More recently he'd also been involved with *Blind Date* and *Gladiators*. In other words, he'd been in the business a long time.

nigel, pick me!

But the inspiration behind the project that would become *Popstars* came to Nigel while he was on holiday. 'I got the idea when my wife, Bonnie, and I were visiting our son, Simon, a director on Australia's Seven Network television channel,' he recalled. 'They were screening a similar show. I watched one episode and I was captivated. I was so desperate to know what would happen that when we had a dinner date the next night, I didn't want to leave the TV. And I was frustrated when we had to fly home and miss the end.'

The idea was not a new one. As far back as the 1960s, television had been interested in putting together a pop act, starting with The Monkees, billed as America's answer to The Beatles. In 1980 the BBC documentary, *The Big Time*, had followed the fortunes of and promoted Sheena Easton, a singer who went on to enjoy international success and to sing the theme song to the James Bond movie, *For Your Eyes Only*.

nothing but hear'say

The Australian series had produced a five-piece all-girl band called Bardot. Their first single became the first debut by an Australian act to enter that country's singles chart at number one. More than a fifth of the Australian population bought it. Bardot's album made similar history, being the first debut album to top the charts.

The Australians had themselves borrowed the idea, from a series on New Zealand TV, that had also led to an all-girl group, called TrueBliss, enjoying brief fame in 1999.

Nigel immediately recognised the potential for the same sort of series in Britain. 'Suddenly, I realised that although I may know the world of auditions inside out, the public didn't and would find it fascinating.' And so *Popstars* was born.

The response to the advert in *The Stage* was immediate. Many heard about it from local newspapers or radio stations. Nearly 3,000

nigel, pick me!

hopefuls turned up at the open auditions around the country. Over the next six weeks, in ten cities, their numbers would be whittled down, until finally a five-piece band would emerge.

To aid Nigel in his quest were two other judges. Paul Adam was Director of A&R (Artists and Repertoire) at Polydor, and had worked with the likes of S Club 7 and Boyzone. Nicki Chapman was the manager of teenage singing sensation Billie Piper, and had been a publicist for The Spice Girls. Both knew the music business inside out. They would accompany Nigel at the auditions and, with him, make the final decision on the eventual line-up of the *Popstars* band. The three of them were agreed on what they were looking for. 'First and foremost, we want vocal talent,' said Nigel. 'They will be five individuals. But to succeed in the band they have got to be complimentary to each other. They have to work together as a band.'

The first episode of *Popstars* was broadcast on January 10 2001, and overnight Nigel became a celebrity – as the person the viewers loved to hate. He was branded 'Nasty Nigel' after 'Nasty Nick', the villain in the previous year's television sensation, *Big Brother*. Nigel earned the title for his cutting remarks and put-downs of some of the more hapless applicants at the auditions. One critic called him 'this strangely lovable reptile.' But the man himself made no apologies for his approach.

'If I'm stood in front of somebody who would not make it in a pop band, and shouldn't even be attempting to sing in the bath, I can't say: "Well done, thank you," and move on,' he said. 'I have to make a statement.' Viewers had to agree that Nigel had a point.

Those auditioning were given a choice of songs. For the girls this included S Club 7's *Reach* and Britney Spears' *Baby One More Time*; for the boys, Ricky Martin's *Livin' La Vida Loca* and Robbie Williams' *Angels*. Nigel and his fellow judges, Paul and Nicki, were to hear these songs over and over again for the next few weeks, and some of the versions bore very little resemblance to the original, to put it kindly.

'Sometimes you think: "What on earth am I doing standing here listening to you attempt to sing this song when you stand absolutely no chance of getting in this band?" ' said Nigel. 'When they sat there for four hours waiting for their turn you would have thought they would have said to themselves: "There are some good singers here – I obviously can't do it."

'But it was amazing the amount of kids who got up there and couldn't sing a note. I was surprised that people would be prepared to show themselves up as they did – they have got to be stupid or deaf. They believe that pop stars are so manufactured that they don't actually sing; they stand there looking pretty and miming.'

Anyone who did think that, or who just didn't come up to scratch, was soon told so in no uncertain terms by Nigel. He said to one contestant: 'You've got the look, you've got the moves, and I'm sure the tune was in there somewhere.' Another was informed: 'I think you misunderstood my question. I asked you to sing it, not speak it.' A female singer who was struggling with her rendition of *My Heart Will Go On*, the theme from the film *Titanic*, asked: 'Can I take it from the bridge?' 'Nasty Nigel' replied: 'You can take it from the bridge or you can take it from the hold, but I can tell you now the ship still sinks in the end.'

Then there was the nervous red-headed youngster at the Glasgow audition who Nigel insisted made another effort at singing *Angels* after he had forgotten the words. Once more, Nigel defended what he had done. 'There was no way I was going to let him go home thinking: "I let myself down,"' he explained.

The contestants came from all corners of the country and from a huge variety of backgrounds. But all of them had the same dream: fame. And even for those who didn't make it, the experience of being in the auditions resolved them to keep trying.

Stuart Pawley, a 22-year-old butcher from Co Durham, was typical. 'I've always loved singing in the car or at work. The customers and my mates are always telling me to shut up. But I have always been very shy and the audition was the first time I had performed in public. It really boosted my confidence. Before then I thought I would be a butcher for life. I want to be the next Robbie Williams – you've got to set your sights high.'

Nikki Maclachlan, aged 19, who worked in a chip shop in Ardrossan in Scotland, came to the auditions having previously won £200 in a singing contest. 'I've always wanted to be in a band and *Popstars* is the best opportunity I'll get. I've been practising my dance routines in front of the mirror.'

For all those who could not sing in key or hold a note, there was also a great deal of talent, as even 'Nasty Nigel' acknowledged. 'It's a bit like going pearl diving,' he said. 'You can open up lots of oysters and find nothing in there, and then you can find one and you go: "Yes, thank you." '

Our first glimpses of the eventual members of the *Popstars* band came during these initial auditions. Contestant number 137 at the Manchester audition was described as 'Kimberley'. She was first seen outside the venue, among a crowd of other hopefuls, telling the camera with a laugh: 'I just want to be on the telly and give it loads!' She performed *My Heart Will Go On* rather more successfully than previous contestants, and the strength of her voice was instantly evident, something which the viewers – and the three judges – noted just as quickly.

Contestant number 27 at the Manchester audition was Suzanne. She also caught everyone's eye with her rendition of S Club 7's *Reach*. 'I think the judges are looking at personality more than anything, maybe looks, and then I'd say the voice was the last thing,' she told the show. 'A lovely little performer,' was Nigel's first reaction upon seeing her. 'You could almost see her in S Club 7,' he said to an equally approving Nicki Chapman.

At the London audition, viewers got their first sight of Danny, performing *Livin' La Vida Loca*. Myleene was also there, and, like Danny, passed through to the next stage.

The final one of the first auditions was held in Cardiff. Here, Noel made an immediate impression on the judges, singing the Santana hit single, *Smooth*. Nicki spoke for Nigel and Paul as well when she said: 'We love Noel.' From the start, he looked a likely candidate to be included in the final band.

Many other talented performers shone through immediately. One was Claire Freeland, from Lanarkshire in Scotland, whose soaring version of *Reach* in her pink cowboy hat was one of the highlights of the early episodes of *Popstars*. She revealed afterwards that she sang regularly in pubs and clubs, and it showed. However, Claire had one concern: that she was too large, and that the judges were looking for slimmer girls. Even so, she easily got through to the next stage: two days of further auditions at Birmingham's National Indoor Arena.

From everyone they had seen, Nigel and his fellow judges had decided on a shortlist of 163 candidates to take to Birmingham. Within 48 hours that number would have shrunk to only 33. As they arrived, they were greeted by Nigel with the words: 'The talented ones are here, and we're grateful you're here.' The assembled youngsters cheered. But Nigel paused. 'The bad news,' he added, 'is that we've got to lose around 130 of you.'

For the next two days, the contestants were split into smaller groups and subjected to more rigorous tests than the first set of auditions. On Day One, they were asked to perform the 1960s Mamas and Papas hit, *Monday Monday*, along with a series of accompanying dance moves. On Day Two, the song was All Saints' *Never Ever*, with another dance routine to learn. And all the time, Nigel, Nicki and Paul scrutinised everyone carefully, listening intently to their voices, watching how they moved, weighing up how each person fitted into being in a group.

At the end of the first day the numbers had been cut to 103 and by early on the second day, the group had been reduced still further to 60. Nicki confronted them. 'Look around you, because the band is in this room.' Once again, Noel stood out. 'Noel has got a good look and, more importantly, he has a great voice as well,' said Nigel. As soon as he was told he was going to the next stage of auditions, Noel called his mother at home in Cardiff – a sight to which viewers were to become accustomed: Noel breaking the good news and then rocking with laughter at his mother's response as she shrieked with delight down the phone, audibly enough to be heard on TV.

On the morning of the second day, however, Kym was far less assured. She had a sore throat, and didn't think she would be able to perform. 'I can't do it,' she claimed. But she did, in a group of five which included Danny, and a tall young Scotsman who was coming to the attention of the judges, and would soon be the highest profile candidate on *Popstars* after the final five who were chosen: Darius.

The two days were over, and the final 33 were selected. As she suspected, Claire from Scotland found that her exceptional voice was not enough. She was out. The survivors were now heading for London and five days of the most intensive tests that any of them had ever faced.

chapter three
Walking The Green Mile

At the rehearsal rooms in London, 15 boys and 18 girls assembled, each knowing that they were now very close to the final line-up of the band. But they also knew, of course, that over the next five days, 28 of them were doomed to failure.

New characters emerged, like Warren from east London, who worked in a bank but dreamed of being a music star. He'd already been recognised by a couple of bank customers from earlier episodes. But he arrived for the final

nothing but hear'say

London auditions suffering from jet lag, after returning from a holiday in Los Angeles.

Darius, meanwhile, was suffering on the first morning from living it up at the welcome party that London Weekend Television had thrown the previous night for the 33 surviving candidates. He was hoping for the day off, but he didn't get that – or any sympathy – from Nigel. 'You did plenty of jumping around and dancing last night,' he told Darius.

On the first day, the contestants practised dance movements with choreographer Di Cook, and harmonies while singing *Bridge Over Troubled Water*, with leading voice coach Annie Skates. Suzanne had a throat infection, but it was something else that was playing on her mind. 'I've got a concern that my weight is a little over what I should be, because looking out there everybody is so slim, and I just feel a little bit conscious of that.'

At the end of the first day in London, the candidates were introduced to an ordeal that would grow worse with each day: the long walk across the main rehearsal room to the desk at the other end, at which sat Nigel, Paul and Nicki. Each day, everyone would be told on these occasions what the judges had thought of their performances and, more importantly, whether they were staying for the next day, or going home. The walk to the desk quickly became known as 'The Green Mile' after the Tom Hanks film of the same name about capital punishment.

Nicki Chapman explained the dilemma that the judges felt. 'It's easy to make the decision,' she said of how they came to choose who stayed and who went. 'It's difficult to explain why, without hurting their feelings and without killing what they've got.' It was a concern that the judges would feel increasingly over the next few nerve-wracking days.

Five candidates were told they would not be coming back for the second day. Darius was not among them, but there was a word of warning to him at his Green Mile discussion from

Nigel. 'There is something about confidence that is different from cockiness,' he was told. It was a warning that Darius was not to heed.

Suzanne awoke on the morning of Day Two in a gloomy state. Her throat was even worse, and that wasn't good for her voice. 'I'm feeling like I'm really going to mess up on the singing today,' she complained, adding: 'I might as well just go home now.'

The judges had more dance routines in store for the candidates on Day Two, as well as vocal work. Everyone was required to perform on their own, singing a song of their choice. Warren was rehearsing his in the toilets beforehand – a gospel song that he often sang at the church he attended. Darius also planned to sing something out of the ordinary: one of his own songs. Suzanne had finally settled on Christina Aguilera's *Genie In A Bottle*, because it would not require her to reach for too many high notes with her sore throat.

The judges were not particularly impressed with any of them. Voice coach Annie Skates complained that Suzanne's performance was too low key; Nicki Chapman asked Warren to sing something more contemporary, reducing him to tears afterwards, and Nigel also wanted Darius to perform something more familiar to the judges. What happened next sealed Darius's fate.

With his characteristic swagger of self-confidence, Darius took the stage and broke into a highly personalised version of *Baby One More Time*, slowing the pace of the song right down, turning high notes into low ones and vice-versa, and finishing with a typically over-exaggerated flourish. His fellow contestants whooped with approval at his audacity. But the three judges did not share their opinion. A bemused looking Paul said: 'He's got talent, but I'm not sure if he's the right sort of person to fit into a five-piece band – even a 100-piece band.'

Nigel was more blunt. 'To do something like he's just done there, which was a complete show-off, that doesn't work, is crazy.' After the *Popstars* series was over, Paul revealed that, unlike Nigel, *he* hadn't liked Darius from the start: 'I didn't trust him. I just thought: "I don't believe in you."

'Nigel wanted him in his five, and I said: "Over my dead body." We would have fallen out about that.' Now they didn't need to; Darius had made their minds up for them. Paul recalled: 'When he did that silly Britney Spears cover, Nigel just said: "You've won, Paul." '

As Darius walked the Green Mile at the end of the second day, he was unaware of what was to come. Nigel didn't waste time or words. 'We do not see you in this pop band and consequently we're not going to ask you back tomorrow.' Darius nodded mutely, but, naturally, still had something to say. 'I will have a triple platinum album by the time I'm 35. I think I have been given a gift and it would be a sin if I didn't share it.' Only Darius could have come out with that.

But Darius was gone – and the rest of the candidates were stunned. Many wept at the news, including Kym, who, like others, had grown close to him, and had believed his talent would carry him all the way to the final band. Nigel summed him up. 'Darius is a survivor in life, and Darius will do whatever Darius has to do to survive, and it wouldn't surprise me if Darius does have a platinum disc within the next five years, and I wish him well in getting it.'

Day Three dawned with Suzanne still sounding worried. 'A part of me says you're nothing less than anyone else out there, give it your all, you've got a chance to get through. Part of me says: "Look around you – look how pretty, look how talented the people are in this room; I couldn't get through this lot." So my confidence is sometimes strong, and sometimes not. I'm just like that all the time.'

She was not alone. Another five contestants had departed along with Darius the previous day. There were now 22 left, and they would know their fate within three days.

However, the third day turned out to offer some respite from the tension. It was spent working on team building exercises to give the judges the opportunity to discover who worked best within a group, and who didn't. Paul noticed that Kym and Suzanne were particularly effective together. The good news for everyone at the end of the day was that there was no Green Mile. Everyone was staying – for the moment.

Kym, however, quickly grasped that this would mean more candidates would be for the chop the following day, and sensibly spent the night in her hotel room working on her harmonies, along with Suzanne, and another contestant called Jessica. Two others were not so conscientious. Raymond and Taz stayed in the hotel bar until the small hours, with Raymond drinking port at the suggestion of Taz, who said it would help his sore throat. It did not prove to be helpful advice.

All the survivors were put through a press conference the next day to see how they would react to media attention. The 'journalists' were, in fact, members of staff at London Weekend Television, but the searching and direct questions they posed were exactly what the eventual *Popstars* band could expect.

One of the toughest questions that they faced concerned drugs. Everyone was asked if they approved of them. Myleene handled the inquiry shrewdly, saying that it was something about which she would prefer not to comment. But Jessica fell into the trap, and admitted that she had once tried cannabis. The fact that she pointed out straight away that she would not use it again and did not approve of it came too late. As it was explained to her afterwards, had the conference been a real one, the press would have seized on her admission and run it on their front pages the following day.

Another eight were told that their services were no longer required as Day Four drew to a close. Jessica, convinced that she would be one of them after her press conference ordeal, broke down in tears when she learned that she was wanted for the final day in London. Her show of emotion caused Nicki to cry.

For Warren and Taz, it was bad news. But the saddest moment came when Raymond was told that he hadn't made it. Paul Adam was visibly upset at having to tell him, and recalled afterwards: 'He walked down the room, sat down, and as I was talking to him this tear, in slow motion, started and rolled down his face, really, really slowly. It was one time that I got completely emotional. I felt really sorry for the guy, shattering his dream.'

Nicki Chapman also found it a traumatic moment. 'We were all fine until we did Raymond and you could just see he was absolutely shattered. You do think: "My God, has he lost what he had because of us?" I really hope not.'

On the morning of the final day, it was suddenly Danny who was plagued with worries. 'I think I might be going today,' he told the cameras. Nicki felt that he was lacking confidence because he appeared to be in awe of everyone else. Nigel swiftly encouraged Danny. 'I need you to get back up there quickly,' he urged him.

Kym summed up the general mood. 'Even though people are laughing and happy and joking, it's all a big front because inside they just feel like crying, because they know somebody's got to go today. You're partly hoping it's not you, but then, if it's not you, you're feeling for the other people that it is. So you have mixed emotions.'

After another full day of practising movement and harmonies – on *Bridge Over Troubled Water* yet again – the time had come. Nigel ushered ten of the final 14 into another rehearsal room, saying that he wanted them to perform another song. In fact, his motive was to tell the four remaining contestants that it was the end of the road for them. Moments later, he informed the ten that they were the ones who had made it. They shrieked and hugged with joy and disbelief.

From the original 3,000 applicants, it had now come to this: ten people who were so close to realising the biggest dream of their lives. But, of course, it was not over yet. The greatest heartbreak was still to come.

chapter four
Welcome To The Band

The judges decided to break the news to the final ten about whether or not they had made the *Popstars* line-up at the candidates' own homes. It was felt to be more appropriate than informing them by telephone or letter. It also made for better television, of course.

More than 12 million viewers tuned in to ITV on the evening of Saturday February 3 2001, to watch the double episode, the first part of which was broadcast at 6.45pm, and the second at 9.15pm. The series had been so successful that ITV had already scheduled extra episodes, and ten million had watched the penultimate one on the previous Wednesday.

The identity of the band had been known within the media for some time because the show was pre-recorded. But the names of the successful five had remained secret. The press had obviously been tempted to name the final line-up, but, with the exception of one Sunday newspaper which published pictures of the band, editors decided not to spoil the surprise, and run the risk of alienating their readers by doing so.

The first to face the verdict was Kevin, from Blackburn, who already sang in a boy band, and had previously appeared on television, too – in *Stars In Their Eyes*. He had performed as Simon Fowler of Ocean Colour Scene, singing their hit *The Riverboat Song*. Kevin was the only one of the ten who was not seen at his home, meeting Nicki in her London office instead.

'It is very difficult for the three judges because in the final ten that we got down to, you saw yourself the talent,' Nicki told Kevin. 'Anybody in that ten could be in the band. We have to get it down to five, so I am saying to you that you haven't made the final five.'

There was a pause as Kevin took in the gravity of what he had just been told. He betrayed little emotion. 'It was difficult,' Nicki reassured him. 'You didn't do anything wrong, that's the truth. We thought all ten of you were great. But what we're looking for is the overall look of the band, the way it works together, the way personalities work together, and we have to be hard and make that final judgement.'

At her parents' home in Wigan, Lancashire, Kym waited nervously for Paul Adam. Her father told her: 'The thing is you've done your best and you've got this far, and we're just happy that you've got this far. Anything else is a bonus.' He knew of course that if Kym was rejected, it wouldn't feel like that.

Paul arrived and, as he settled himself in the front room, asked Kym how she felt. She replied that she hadn't been able to sleep for the past few nights, especially the previous night. Paul was in no hurry to put her out of her misery.

'Obviously we're down to the last ten and it's very tough for us now,' he said. 'Everyone's got such strong voices now and good personalities so . . .' Paul left the 'so' hanging in the air for a few seconds, though it seemed much longer, especially to Kym. 'I'm afraid . . . you're going to have to move down to London for a few months and join the group.' Kym screamed with delight and, not least, at the release of tension. It had been clear from the look on her face when Paul uttered the words 'I'm afraid' that for one awful moment, Kym had thought she'd failed.

One of the most emotional moments of this charged *Popstars* episode came when Nigel Lythgoe knocked on the door of the Newcastle home of Michelle. She had been in this situation before, reaching the final 12 in the selection process for a band called Girl Thing. She sat tensely with her parents on either side of her, and Nigel in front of her.

'I know you don't want me to beat around the bush, because the judges' decision is important to you, so I won't,' he told her. 'I'm afraid you haven't been chosen for the band and I'm sorry.'

For a moment Michelle remained composed. Then, pointing out the bottle of champagne which remained unopened nearby, awaiting Nigel's verdict, her mother said: 'We're still going to have a glass of champagne to celebrate, because she got this far and we're really proud she's got this far.' It was then that Michelle's face crumpled, and she dissolved into tears.

'It was a tough decision,' said Nigel, trying to find words to comfort her. 'We looked at everybody. There was not one person that we could have said was not right for the band in that last ten.' Michelle was evidently not convinced. 'Pick yourself up, dust yourself off, and start all over again,' Nigel urged her quietly. 'I don't know if I have got the energy to do it again,' whispered Michelle.

Next was Suzanne, who also awaited Nigel, at her grandmother's house in her hometown of Bury, Lancashire. After greeting her family, Nigel's face became serious. 'I will be totally honest with you – you split the judges' decision,' he said. 'You split us two and one. Two went for one girl and one went for another, and the one was eventually persuaded to go with the other two, and I think everyone was delighted with the eventual decision.'

welcome to the band

Still he didn't reveal whether or not Suzanne had reached the final five. Then he handed her a small bag. 'The other judges have sent up this for you and we hope you'll like it.' Suzanne took the gift, looking slightly bemused, and began to open it. 'It's the keys to the house, welcome to the band,' Nigel finally announced.

The other girl whom one of the judges had initially wanted in the band in preference to Suzanne turned out to be Kelli, a superb singer from London. On their meeting at Kelli's flat, Nicki told her: 'You are an absolute star and we very much see you as a solo artist.' As Nicki had previously told Kevin, what was plain was that the judges regarded the look of the band and how its members fitted in with each other as at least as important as how each person sounded.

Noel had a longer wait than most to hear the news. He had been expecting a visit from Nigel, only to be told that Nigel had been delayed in Ireland by bad weather, where he had been meeting another of the final ten, Tony. Noel was informed that Paul Adam would be coming the following day – at noon. Paul eventually turned up eight hours late.

'It has been tough with the guys to differentiate because of the quality of the voices,' Paul told Noel, and it looked as if he was going to keep him hanging on for the answer as he had earlier with Kym. But Noel had waited long enough. Paul told him simply: 'You're in.' Moments later, Noel's mother burst in after being told the news to hug both Noel and Paul, and let out another of the sort of shrieks which viewers had previously only heard coming down the phone after one of Noel's calls to her.

At his home in London, with his mother, aunt and grandmother waiting in the kitchen,

welcome to the band

Danny ushered Nicki into the front room. 'It is very difficult to make sure that we find the right mix,' she told him. 'I think Nigel, Paul and I have found that right mix, and I am pleased to say that you are one of the five.' While obviously delighted, Danny remained as calm and easy-going as he had appeared throughout the auditions. 'I just want to say thanks for this opportunity,' he told Nicki, hugging her.

Now there was only one remaining berth in the band. Three candidates remained: Jessica in Preston, Lancashire, whom Paul went to see; Tony in Ireland, where Nigel headed, and Myleene, who although from Norfolk originally, arranged to meet Nicki at the Royal Academy of Music in London.

'You have made it to the final five.' The person speaking was Nicki, and the last member of the band to be revealed was Myleene.

nothing but hear'say

The *Popstars* band was chosen. Five people, the youngest of whom was 19 and the eldest 24, had suddenly become among the most instantly recognisable faces in Britain thanks to the success of the television programme that discovered them – and that was before they had brought out a single or even come up with a name for their new band. So who exactly were they?

chapter five
Kym

By becoming a *Popstar*, Kym wasn't just realising her own long cherished fantasy, she was also living out the dreams once held by her father.

Long before Kimberley Marsh was born on June 13 1976, in Haydock, near Wigan in Lancashire, her dad, David, had his own band, called Ricky and The Dominant Four. They performed all over the north-west of England, appearing alongside leading acts of the time such as The Shadows and Cilla Black.

The band also played gigs at the legendary Cavern Club in Liverpool in the early 1960s, and even on occasion supported The Beatles before the Fab Four went on to global fame. And the performing tradition in the family went back further. Kym's grandmother on her dad's side, May, had been a singer in the 1950s under the stage name Trudy Scott.

Her parents both quickly noticed that Kym was musical. 'The desire to perform was always there,' said her mum, Pauline. 'From the age of three she would pick up a hairbrush and sing. She'd say: "I'm going to be on *Top Of The Pops* when I'm a big lady." '

'She always sang as a child,' said her dad, 'ever since she could open her mouth. We used to go to a local labour club of a Sunday lunchtime. Kimberley always pestered me to let her get up and sing.

'Finally I gave in. Everyone was amazed when she started singing *Livin' Doll*. No one could believe how good she was.' Pauline added:

myleene daring noel danny

suzanne

myleene danny noel
suzanne

and the future...?

"what on earth is going on?" It's all so amazing what has happened to us in a few months.'

Kym doesn't want to even think about how long Hear'say might last. 'I'd be crazy to do that. The thought hasn't even entered my head. We know that nothing lasts forever but we're going to do our best to stay around for as long as possible – at least a few years. Really, that depends on the public.' The public, meanwhile, show no signs of wanting the *Popstars* fairytale to end just yet.

cancer. 'Luke has been ill but the focus on me in *Popstars* has meant Luke is living through me. That's giving him hope and encouragement. My family are what's important. I'm not doing this for selfish reasons – I want to be able to look after them.' Myleene said: 'When I get the money I'm going to buy my mum and dad a house because I miss them horrendously and I want to make sure they're OK. I owe them everything.'

It was no surprise when Hear'say's second single, *The Way To Your Love*, became another huge hit for the band. Their first nationwide tour kicked off in Noel's home city of Cardiff, and was a sell-out immediately. The band are already working on tracks for a second album, and there have been talks with ITV about various ideas for programmes, including a Christmas special called *A Very Hear'say Christmas* and a series which would look back at their first year together.

So, can the Hear'say phenomenon continue? Myleene said: 'Our only race now is against ourselves. I still stop and think sometimes:

a bloke came up and asked me to buy him a pair of £130 Nike trainers! He thought that was a drop in the ocean for me because the papers said we were worth £3 million. I couldn't believe his cheek. You couldn't print what I said to him!'

Certainly there had been much speculation about what the members of Hear'say might earn. It was pointed out that over five years each of The Spice Girls had amassed personal fortunes of an estimated £20 million. Yet Hear'say's first album sold nearly three times as many copies in its first week as The Spice Girls' debut album had managed.

Each of the band members intends to spend at least some of whatever money they earn on their families and relatives. Kym sees it as a way of giving her children the opportunities in life that she didn't have, while Noel's thoughts are with his cousin, Luke, who is suffering from

we've had unwelcome guests too.' The house was burgled three times during their stay.

There had been some very strange moments, too, for Hear'say since they became household names. 'You do have to do reality checks,' says Danny. 'Noel and I went to do a radio interview at the BBC and Fergie was there, you know – the Duchess of York! And she said: "Congratulations." She knew who we were! Noel and I were just thinking: "How bizarre is that?" '

'We didn't know it was going to be this big,' admitted Noel. 'It's freaky to think that you can get off the train anywhere in Britain and people will know who you are.' Each member of the band had similar experiences to recount. 'I was in a restaurant in Paris and this girl asked if I was in Hear'say,' said Kym. 'When I said I was she started bawling – because she was so happy. A few months ago, no one would have noticed. When some people come to our signings they cry or start shaking.'

Danny said: 'I was buying some trainers and

and the future...?

The band had to get used to life without the television series, which had ended once they reached No.1 with *Pure and Simple*. The film crew, particularly the cameraman, had grown close to Hear'say over the months and Kym admitted that she cried at his departure. 'I felt really stupid afterwards – I mean, I should have been relieved to finally have got rid of him! I've finally got a bit of my life back.' Myleene commented: 'The TV programme has given us a great launch pad and it's up to us now.'

They moved out of the house in north London which they had shared since the band was formed. In some ways this was a relief, as it had been visited by hundreds of fans, many of whom rang the doorbell at all times of day and night. 'Most of the time they leave us flowers or want autographs,' said Myleene. 'Some of them write: "We love Hear'say" in the gravel outside. But

'I'll talk about how they appeal to all teenagers,' said Charlotte. 'I spoke to Noel and Danny and Kym and Suzanne. Noel is my heart-throb and I really hope I can meet him one day.'

Charlotte's enthusiasm was a sign of how far Hear'say had come in such a short space of time. But this phenomenon had become apparent to the five from the moment that the line-up of the band was revealed, as Noel found out on a shopping trip in London soon afterwards.

'When Danny and I went to Oxford Street, people were walking past and then shouting: "*Popstars!*" We got stopped by one person and suddenly there was a crowd. It really hit home then.'

After *Pure and Simple* went to No.1, the band took part in a live web chat. Within an hour, 60,000 fans had emailed them with questions. The band even inspired a tribute band called Near'say, featuring five people who certainly resemble the real *Popstars*.

and the future ...?

chapter twelve
And The Future ...?

Not everyone in the music business was as uncomplimentary about Hear'say's rise to fame. Singing star Charlotte Church, who was brought up near Noel's home in Cardiff, admitted that she was a fan of the band and the series that discovered them. 'In fact, I'm even doing my English oral exam on *Popstars*,' she said. 'I was going to do something intellectual like "How philosophy affects our everyday lives" but I thought the class would enjoy this subject far more!

had been chosen by a similar method on a television series in Canada, where she was on tour, she said: 'It makes pop music look in a very bad state because it's so contrived and manufactured. The kids in the groups are very talented but the people behind them are exploiting them.'

But nothing could detract from the band's amazing early success. After the endless work and pressure of the past few months, the five went their separate ways on much deserved holidays. The difference with previous holidays they'd been on was that this time they were going, and returning, as real-life pop stars.

Pure and Simple holding on to the top slot for a third week in the singles chart, it meant that Hear'say had made history, as the first British band to be at No.1 in both the singles and album charts simultaneously with their debut releases.

There was still criticism from certain quarters however. Record producer Pete Waterman, who had guided Kylie Minogue, Jason Donovan and others to success in the late 1980s, called Hear'say 'a group of over-exposed karaoke singers' and predicted that they would soon be forgotten. Lee Latchford-Evans of Steps claimed that the band had achieved their fame too easily because of the television series, even though he and the rest of Steps were themselves chosen through auditions after a magazine advert.

Mel C of The Spice Girls said that she thought Hear'say's success was 'a big publicity stunt.' Asked about Hear'say and a group who

The band were now more popular than any of them had dared to hope. Europe's biggest shopping centre, the vast Bluewater complex in Kent, had to cancel a planned visit by Hear'say because its owners feared that they would never be able to cope with the thousands of fans expected to converge on the mall. Then the biggest book store in the continent, Waterstone's in London's Piccadilly, was forced to take similar action at the last minute when it became evident that a planned autograph-signing session would be impossible to organise because of the numbers expected to turn up.

For the launch of their album, appropriately called *Popstars*, 5,000 fans crowded out Coventry city centre to greet the band. The album came out only a fortnight after the release of *Pure and Simple*, and the response was the same. In only six days, *Popstars* had sold 306,631 copies. It was the biggest ever first week sale for a debut album, beating the first album sales of the likes of Oasis, Craig David and even The Spice Girls. And with that dreams can come true,' Myleene declared. 'We would have been happy with any chart position,' claimed Noel. 'This is the icing on the cake. Five months ago no one knew who we were. We are absolutely privileged to be in this position.' A delighted Danny added: 'This is the biggest adventure of my life, and getting to No.1 fulfils my ultimate ambition and proves people like our music.' Among the congratulations was a message all the way from Borneo, where Nigel Lythgoe was still filming *Survivor*. 'I'm absolutely delighted with the success. It was nothing more than you deserve,' he told them.

Only two charity singles, Band Aid's *Do They Know It's Christmas?* in 1984 and Elton John's *Candle in the Wind* tribute to Diana, Princess of Wales in 1997, had sold more copies than *Pure and Simple* in its first week. Sales had already reached 550,000 – smashing the previous record for a debut single, which had been held by Britney Spears' *Baby One More Time*. That had sold 463,000 in February 1999.

very nervous time for them because it could all have so easily gone wrong if no one had turned up. As it was, they were simply overwhelmed by the response.'

The scenes were repeated later in the week at a Woolworth's store in Milton Keynes, Buckinghamshire. This time the place was packed out with more than 8,000 autograph hunters. Police had to turn away thousands of fans who had queued for hours simply because they feared that they might otherwise be crushed.

So by the time the live Sunday episode came around, the question of who would be No.1 was a foregone conclusion. Presenter Davina McCall joined the five at their north London home for the Radio 1 chart countdown, to hear DJ Mark Goodier confirm that they had made it.

The band hugged each other and the family members who had joined them for the celebrations. 'It is completely unbelievable but we have all wanted it so badly and it is living proof

store HMV, said: 'I think we are already looking at the song which will be this year's biggest selling single.'

The final episode of *Popstars* was due to be shown live on ITV the following Sunday, and the idea was that the band would discover on air whether *Pure and Simple* had made it to No.1. As a result, their record company were hoping to keep the good news from the five, so that their reaction could be filmed live. But they got a rather conclusive clue to their popularity when they turned up at the Oxford Street HMV store in London on the day of the single's release.

Around 3,500 fans besieged the store to catch a glimpse of the band at their first public signing session. Some had waited more than nine hours for them to arrive. A spokesman for Hear'say told newspapers: 'This was their first chance to meet the public one to one. It was a

'That really hit us all when we went home for the first time after joining the band,' said Myleene. 'We all cried because we knew things had changed forever. But it's not you who changes. It's everything and everyone around you.'

Their choice of first single, *Pure and Simple*, had originally been meant for a band called Girl Thing. But the songwriters – who included early 1990s singer, Betty Boo – decided instead to sell it to Hear'say. It was immediately well received by newspaper critics, one of whom called it 'surprisingly catchy' and 'sophisticated.' But would the record-buying public react to it?

The answer was not long in coming. On the first day of its release, *Pure and Simple* sold an astonishing 160,995 copies. To put that figure in perspective, The Spice Girls' biggest selling hit, *2 Become 1*, sold only 34,000 on its first day. Meanwhile, the song that was at No.1 at the time, Westlife's *Uptown Girl*, had sold just 43,000. Gennaro Castaldo, a chart expert for the record

chapter eleven
Pure And Simple

With the *Popstars* series coming to an end on television, and their single about to released, Danny, Myleene, Kym, Noel and Suzanne all returned home to see families and friends, their lives transformed. 'Going home made me realise things are never going to be the same,' said Noel, who was filmed breaking down briefly as he returned to Cardiff. 'We are always going to be the *Popstars* even if the group doesn't succeed. We hadn't let it out yet and it just got to me.'

they're idiots. Do it for the fans," ' said Kym. The song Hear'say performed at the Brits was to be their first single: *Pure and Simple*.

'What is amazing is that, last year, I was watching the Brits with a can of beer and a Chinese meal. I never dreamed I'd be on the stage a year later.'

The reception they received from the audience suggested that some people thought Hear'say had had it too easy, and were not the real thing. For among the many cheers, there were a few boos and whistles, including some from other bands. But the five were not deterred.

'I wasn't nervous at all being up there alongside U2 and Craig David. It felt right, but we were honoured to be there,' said Danny. A typically confident Myleene claimed: 'If we weren't such a threat, I think they'd have found it easier to let go, have a sense of humour, and clap us.'

And there was sympathy for them from at least one very influential source: Robbie Williams. 'He came up to us after we were booed, and said: "Don't worry about them,

was. It had a big round face,' she complained.

Hear'say finally made their long awaited first public performance, and – to the surprise of everyone who had heard the strength of their voices during the making of *Popstars* – they mimed. Appearing on Channel 5's *Pepsi Chart Show*, they pretended to sing along to a tape. Their record label later claimed that it was because backing tracks had not been ready in time for live vocals.

However, the public did not have long to wait to hear the real thing. Hear'say went on ITV's *SM:tv*, to be introduced by Ant and Dec before performing *The Way To Your Love*, and this time they were singing. The following evening, they sang live again: at the prestigious Brit Awards.

It was a nerve-wracking moment for the five, and a stark illustration of how far they had come in such a short time. As Danny pointed out:

considered and discarded before the final choice was made, including Bubble Wrap and Mixed Race. So why Hear'say? Kym explained: 'We were reading a magazine and, because of all the kiss-and-tell stories going on about us, we thought: "That's really cool." '

The band's workload had become more hectic than ever. There were photographic shoots to attend, interviews to give to magazines, radio stations and television programmes, and dance routines to master. They were frequently getting only three or four hours of sleep a night.

One of the projects which the band found strangest to be involved with was the Hear'say dolls, for which they modelled. Noel thought his was uncannily lifelike. 'Mine was just like me. It even had that little bit of flesh here,' he said, pointing to his chin. Kym, in particular, wasn't happy with hers. 'I couldn't believe how ugly mine

This was an issue that the girls in the band felt passionately about. Myleene said: 'It's a fight to prove how normal we are. We crave cheeseburgers, pizzas and chocolate. We will never be size eights and I feel very strongly about this. It's an important issue because we are real girls. People can relate to us, and I'm not going to make myself ill to please somebody else.'

Nigel said goodbye to the band shortly afterwards. He was travelling to an island in the Far East to make a new television series, called *Survivor*. By now, the five had realised the importance of having a manager to look after the business side of their affairs. They chose Chris Herbert, who had in the past created The Spice Girls and Five.

The band came up with a name at last, too: Hear'say. Various suggestions had been

admission to Nigel, who assured her that it was not a problem and that she would have been chosen for the band anyway.

And then there was the moment when Nigel mentioned Kym's weight. 'What happened was this,' Kym remembered. 'I'd been given diet sheets from the doctor to pass around the group, and she had said that we all needed to get fit and that we could stand to lose some weight. When I told Nigel, he said: "No, I think it's just you who needs to lose weight. Christmas is over, Kym, and the goose is still fat."'

In one of the series' most memorable scenes, Kym stormed furiously out of the room. What Nigel was not aware of at that point, of course, was the problem with her weight that Kym had had in her teens.

'What Nigel said was very hurtful,' she said. 'I had put on a couple of pounds, but who doesn't at Christmas? And to be told in front of 11 million viewers! It's bad enough to be told in front of friends, but I am not overweight.'

reporters awaited the five as they flew back from recording in Norway to face their first press conference as a band, at Heathrow airport. There had been changes while they had been away. Suzanne had added blonde hair extensions, and Kym had red highlights in her hair.

Kym admitted that they approached their return to Britain with some trepidation. 'We haven't got a clue what's going on in the real world because we've been in hiding,' she said. 'We can't feel the buzz surrounding the show yet. We're being filmed every day saying: "We're doing this" and we still don't know whether anyone actually cares.'

Millions did care, of course, and not least because of Kym. It was revealed in the newspapers that she had two children, something she had kept hidden from the *Popstars* judges. She was seen in one of the series' episodes making a tearful

February 3, the day of the double episode in which viewers discovered the five's identities, *The Times* authoritatively informed its readers: 'the group is to be named Inner Spin.'

They were already having to get used to the criticism that they were manufactured by a television series, and not a 'real' band. Virgin Radio, owned by Chris Evans, announced that it would not play the band's first single. Darius, whose audition performances had turned him into a television star overnight, declared of the *Popstars* line-up: 'I think they are in danger of being just a flash in the pan.' Kelli, Jessica, Michelle, Tony and Kevin – the five rejected at the last minute by the *Popstars* judges – announced that they were to form their own band, called Liberty.

Suzanne said it was up to them to prove doubters wrong. 'Yes, we're manufactured in the sense that we had to audition to make it into the band, but now we're together the rest is up to us. If the public don't like us, it's our own fault.'

Dozens of newpaper and television

photographers were starting to hang around locations at which they thought they might be able to take pictures of the band and reveal who they were before the series did. The five had to resort to wearing joke masks when they went out in public together.

On one occasion, they were invited along by Nigel Lythgoe to the recording of *An Audience With Ricky Martin* at London Weekend Television studios. At a party afterwards they mingled with celebrity guests, and whenever anyone asked who the five were, they were told that they were competition winners, whose prize had been the chance to attend the recording.

Even before their names became public, bookmakers were quoting odds of only 2-1 on the *Popstars* band – whoever they were – having a No.1 with their first single, and 6-1 that they would have the Christmas No.1. On

ordered by the band to wear socks at all times rather than wander around barefoot!' she said.

'Their lives have changed just like that,' said Nigel Lythgoe of the five. 'The most difficult thing is going to be that the public think they own them. A few weeks from now they will be recognised wherever they go – they have yet to experience that.'

In the meantime, the band faced a huge amount of work in a short amount of time. They went to studios in Sheffield and London, and travelled to Norway for a week, each time recording tracks for their first album, one of which would be their first single. They had only eight weeks to record an album which would normally take six months.

Meanwhile, the press speculated on their identities. *Popstars* had quickly become one of the most watched series on television, and as a result

The house, in north London, was bigger and more luxurious than anything the five had ever experienced before. There was a large drawing room and lounge downstairs, with a conservatory and a music and dance studio, that contained a piano and a mirrored wall. Just inside the front door, there was a plaque. It read: 'Coming together is a beginning. Keeping together is progress. Working together is success.'

The five of them soon decided who was good at what. Not surprisingly for a former office cleaner, Danny did a lot of the housework. Noel took charge of the cooking, and Myleene was the organiser, taking charge of dealing with the record company, television producers and lawyers, until they appointed a manager.

They also had to get used to each other's personal habits. Suzanne spent every spare moment on her mobile phone to her boyfriend or family. Danny was woken every night by Noel getting up and sleepwalking. And worst of all was Kym's feet. 'They're incredibly smelly. I've been

from popstars to hear'say

chapter ten
From Popstars To Hear'say

From the moment the five members of the new *Popstars* band stepped over the threshold of the home they were to share together, they left their old lives behind for ever. They would remain there for the next few weeks until the television series at last revealed their identities.

Noel and Danny immediately agreed to share a room and, after tossing a coin, Myleene and Kym ended up in the second double bedroom, while Suzanne moved into the single room.

nothing but hear'say

Five months after her disappointment over *Coronation Street*, Suzanne, who had now dropped the 'Crow' part of her surname, read the advert in *The Stage* newspaper. She was about to get down to another shortlist, with a happier ending this time.

arts at college in Oldham. She also worked at Oldham's Theatre Workshop, which has produced many of the stars of *Coronation Street*.

But after a year, Suzanne gave up the performing arts course, having joined an Abba tribute band called The Right Stuff. They travelled up and down the country, appearing at clubs and hotels, wedding receptions and on ferry cruises. The band even toured Dubai. Suzanne also began dating her fellow band member, Andrew Warner, who is 16 years her senior.

She still had her eye on an acting career, but was turned down after coming close to getting roles in the soaps, *Emmerdale* and *Coronation Street*. In the latter, Suzanne narrowly missed out on playing Maria, Tyrone Dobbs' girlfriend.

'She was so disappointed not to get the part,' said her dad, Vinnie. 'She thought she might really be in with a chance after she got down to the last two or three. I told her: "Something better could be just around the corner." And boy, was it!'

success did bring her to the attention of school bullies. 'These girls were very jealous,' said Janet. 'She was never precocious or big-headed but some of her classmates just couldn't handle it. It was horrible. She tried to avoid them but they always found her.'

Small parts followed in other television series, including *Holby City* on BBC1, and the police drama *City Central* on the same channel. She'd also appeared in a commercial for petroleum company Esso, doing the splits on roller skates to the slogan: 'That's low, but not as low as Esso prices.' At the time, Suzanne became a huge fan of teen idols, Take That. But it wasn't Robbie Williams whom she had a crush on, but Howard Donald. Years later, she would meet him after joining the *Popstars* band, and tell him: 'I even camped outside your house just to catch a glimpse of you.'

Despite her television appearances, Suzanne did not neglect her school work. She left at 16 with nine GCSEs, and studied performing

played Sebastian the Crab. I was a chubby kid and there's a picture of me with a fat orange face, a tight lycra outfit, and big claws. If that ever gets out, I'll kill somebody!'

Another role in the musical *Showboat*, at the Palace Theatre, Manchester, soon followed. Suzanne's voice amazed teachers at her school, where she appeared in a production of *Grease*, and soon came to the attention of artistic director Anthony Williams. 'She just stood out,' he recalled, 'and it was obvious even at 12 that she was going to make it.'

He swiftly signed Suzanne up for performance classes at his studios, to develop her confidence further in front of cameras and on stage. His instincts were quickly proved correct. Suzanne won the lead part in a major BBC science fiction drama for children, called *Elidor*. 'That was wicked,' she said. 'To get on TV at only 12 was the most amazing thing. I got the odd comment at school, but it didn't worry me.'

Her mum confirmed that Suzanne's

walk, she became accustomed to being filmed by her dad Vinnie's video camera. He said: 'Suzanne's always enjoyed performing, ever since she was three and went on stage in a dance competition. She has always looked good on camera because she has grown up with it.'

Suzanne Crowshaw was born on September 29 1981, and spent her early years in a three-bedroomed terrace house in Radcliffe, near Bury in Lancashire. Her mum, Janet, is a district nurse; her dad, Vinnie, runs a video recording business, and Paul, her elder brother by four years, is a laboratory technician.

She was only four when she landed her first professional role, as Molly in the musical, *Annie*. 'I'd audition for school shows, amateur dramatics, anything I could, really,' said Suzanne. 'I also did a lot of dancing competitions which Dad has on video. Once, we did *The Little Mermaid* and I

chapter nine
Suzanne

While all the members of the *Popstars* band started young, probably none of them was destined to be a performer from as early an age as Suzanne. Amazingly, she was only three when she announced to her parents that she wanted to go to Hollywood.

Her mum, Janet, said: 'I've always known Suzanne would be a star. As a tiny child she begged us to let her go to dance lessons.' It probably helped that from the moment she could

For his mum, Claire, it was a wrench to see Noel leave home. 'I was adopted and Noel's dad didn't really have anything to do with him, so we stuck together,' she said. 'We're both "take-us-as-you-find-us" people who like to laugh. The programme made him out to be a mummy's boy, but he only keeps in touch – like the rest of the *Popstars*.'

Eventually Noel returned to Wales. 'I just woke up one morning and decided to come home and go for every audition I could,' he said. Once again, he found himself working as a waiter, this time in a Latin American cafe in Cardiff, and saving up to move down to London.

Then a friend of his mum's tipped him off about the *Popstars* auditions after reading about them in the local newspaper. Noel was off to London sooner than he thought.

tion as a joker. 'He was always making us laugh and playing jokes on people. He got us free chocolate dessert after every meal by telling each waitress it was his birthday. It worked every time.'

Back in Cardiff, Noel began touring pubs and clubs in south Wales with a female impersonator act, as a backing singer. One of the shows involved him dressing as a daffodil, and the picture of him in the costume was published soon after he found fame on *Popstars*.

'It was a Welsh theme, so I dressed as a daffodil,' Noel explained. 'Another lad dressed as a leek and another as a rugby player. I got the short straw. The daffodil pictures are now under lock and key at my mum's house.'

He also spent two summers working on the Spanish holiday resort island of Ibiza. Noel sang at the Millennium Bar on the island, owned by Dawn Allen. She said: 'He's the next Robbie Williams. He's got a great voice. He's brilliant at ballads. I used to say to the customers he'd go on to be a big star.'

At around about the same time, Noel began working as a waiter to earn money, a job that he was to return to over the next few years. 'I've done it on and off since I was 16 and absolutely hated it,' he said later. 'I was always spilling food and the only thing I liked was meeting people. Apart from that it was like pulling teeth.'

But he did also begin to see the world for the first time. Noel joined a Welsh male voice choir, called Only Men Aloud, and travelled with them on a two and a half month tour of the east coast of the United States, singing hymns and classical numbers at 44 venues.

Fellow chorister Tim Rhys-Evans said: 'When he sang, the hairs on the back of my neck stood up. His voice literally gave you the goose bumps. Once, after he'd finished a solo, the audience were spellbound. You could have heard a pin drop. Then there was this rapturous applause.'

Another friend in the choir, Huw Farmer, recalled how Noel was already gaining a reputa-

when he appeared in his school's nativity play, and stopped it halfway through the performance. Noel said: 'All the mothers were crying and you couldn't hear a thing.' So the youngster stomped to the front of the stage. 'I just told them all I wouldn't sing if they didn't stop blubbing.'

Noel also had to contend with his parents separating while he was still young. But he claimed that this and the deaths of his brother and sister helped toughen him up. 'Going through experiences like that so young sets you up for later on in life.'

After attending St John's Cathedral School and then his local comprehensive school in Cardiff, Noel went to St David's College in the city, where he took English, Media Studies and Drama A-levels. The college's head of drama, Richard Tunley, said of Noel: 'He was thirsty for performance and always got very involved on the practical and social side of productions. Once he took a small part in a play, but he was the one people were talking about afterwards.'

story of personal tragedy. For when Noel was aged six, his six-month-old baby brother, Dominic, was a cot death victim, and three years later, his baby sister, Alicia-Monique, died aged only nine days old, from a brain tumour. And Noel's family still lives under the shadow of illness: his young cousin, Luke, has cancer.

Noel Sullivan was born on July 28 1980, and was brought up in the Cardiff suburb of Ely. His family, too, had a musical background. His grandmother on his mother's side, Monique, was a professional cellist and music teacher, who moved to Cardiff before Noel's mum, Claire, was born.

Claire, a nurse, recalled that Noel could sing before he could speak. 'He couldn't say a full sentence, but he could sing. Some boys love football. Noel loved to sing.'

His first starring role came at the age of five

chapter eight
Noel

From the earliest episodes of *Popstars*, Noel became a favourite with the viewers. He was good looking, it was instantly apparent that he could sing, and his telephone calls home to his mother – and her shrieks down the line as he told her he'd passed the latest audition – became one of the most eagerly awaited parts of the series.

But behind the laughter and the obvious affection between mother and son lay a

TV presenter Lily Savage that Myleene first found out about the *Popstars* auditions, which were taking place next door. She had nearly missed them. 'It seemed from the *Popstars* programme that I'd arrived two days late and didn't really care, but they were saying there were no places left and I was desperate for them to accept me.

'Initially I thought it would be 16-year-olds jumping around to bubblegum pop, which goes against every ethic I have as a musician,' said Myleene, who showed up for the auditions with her brother and sister in tow. 'But I saw that they were doing it and trying to get it right.'

Meanwhile, her former music teacher, Matthew Hardy, was curious to know what the girl who used to be his star pupil was doing these days. 'I phoned Bong at Christmas and she said Myleene had been very busy, but didn't say what she was doing. Usually she tells me so I was quite suspicious.' With the new *Popstars* series about to start, he and the rest of the country were about to find out.

for her. After the show, I was screaming at the stage door,' he joked.

Then the Royal Academy of Music offered Myleene a post-graduate course, despite the fact that she did not have a university degree which was usually required. She studied opera, and then music theatre. But that didn't mean she was intending to stay in classical music.

'I wanted the classical foundation but even when I was training in opera I wanted to be a pop singer. The classical groups said it was a terrible waste and I'd strain my voice. But locking myself in a room to practise for eight hours a day just wasn't for me.'

After finishing at the Royal Academy of Music, Myleene found work as a backing singer to a number of famous names. They included the Canadian country singer KD Lang, for whom she provided backing vocals on the BBC chat show, *Parkinson*, and Sir Cliff Richard, whom she backed on his No.1 song, *Millennium Prayer*.

But it was while working in the studio with

chance. I got the distinct feeling no one messed with Myleene and got away with it. She was on a mission and no one was going to stand in her way.'

Matthew Hardy agreed. 'When she was 16, and her friends were going out and having fun, she was working,' he says. 'She realised her career was more important.'

In fact, Myleene was so single-minded that she even turned down an offer of a place at Cambridge University to study English or Music. Instead, she went to the training school for the West End musical, *Miss Saigon*. She landed a role in the chorus, after turning down another offer, this time to appear in a touring production of *Jesus Christ Superstar*. So, as she was to explain later: 'I didn't come out of nowhere. I've been doing this job for a while. I got a taste for it, but I never actually got to do it as me.'

Nor did she forget her former music teacher, sending Matthew Hardy tickets for *Miss Saigon* when she got the part. 'I was so pleased

'She was just so very interested. She has a lot of ability and such a strong voice, which she worked tremendously hard on. Myleene's sister, Jessie, also had a lovely voice and they used to sing in harmony. That's quite difficult for a child of her age, but Myleene mastered it.' Even the family's telephone answering machine had a musical message on it sung by the three Klass children, asking callers to leave their number.

By her teens, Myleene was performing in school concerts and church festivals, and helping her music teacher, Matthew Hardy, put together musical arrangements for soloists. She also successfully applied to attend Saturday classes at the London Guildhall School of Music.

It was by now evident that Myleene wouldn't let anything get in the way of her musical ambitions. One of her friends at the time, Kirsty Lewis, recalled: 'Once we went out on a double date to see a film. We missed the movie because the boys were late and I remember Myleene saying that her date had missed his

friends as 'Bong'. Myleene has a younger sister, Jessie, who is a television producer, and a brother, Don, who is an actor.

From the age of four, Myleene began to learn the piano and the violin, and at 11, she took up the harp. 'It was never difficult to get her to practise,' her piano teacher, Dorothy Wright, said later. 'I would watch this little girl play, and just know I was nurturing a huge talent.'

The whole family shared Myleene's passion for music, especially singing. They rapidly earned the nickname 'the Von Trapps' in their home town of Gorleston, Norfolk, after the singing family in the film, *The Sound Of Music*. At the age of ten, Myleene and her younger brother and sister formed the Klass Family Singers, and every Christmas put on a local show.

'They became a regular feature of school concerts,' said their former music master at St Mary's Roman Catholic School, Matthew Hardy. 'They would sing together as a trio. They would even come up with their own arrangements.

chapter seven
Myleene

Myleene Klass was always going to be a musician. However, for many years it seemed certain that her future lay in performing classical music, not as a member of a pop band.

She was born in Great Yarmouth, Norfolk, on April 6 1978, the daughter of Otto, an Austrian merchant seaman, who often spent weeks away at sea, and Magdalena, her half-Filipino, half-Spanish mother, who came to Britain in the 1970s, and is known to family and

message, I must say it was the tackiest thing I'd heard,' he admitted. 'I seriously wondered if I should do it.' Luckily for him, he finally decided he should.

realise his dreams, Danny reasoned that he could always go into the teaching career for which he'd trained.

There was, however, one brief moment when it looked as if Danny didn't have a future of any kind. At the age of 18, he nearly died. 'I had internal bleeding and collapsed in the middle of the night,' recalled Danny. 'My Grandad Reg found me. I was rushed to hospital and lost six pints of blood. It was caused by a bug and it was touch and go.

'It changed my life completely and I started thinking about things more positively. You realise what you take for granted.'

Yet despite his new positive outlook, Danny was not filled with enthusiasm when he spotted the *Popstars* audition advert. He was suffering from flu at the time, but that wasn't the real reason. 'When I phoned and heard the recorded

to sing every Friday night in the pub and loads of people would come up and say: "You're really good."'

One of his teachers from college, Nicky Price, was also impressed: 'He was very focused, very determined, and it was clear that he would go far. Everyone here is absolutely thrilled at his success.'

Asked afterwards what his biggest regret was, Danny replied: 'Not realising that I could sing earlier on. I wish I could have gone to stage school and then I might have had more confidence.' Nonetheless, after finishing his college course, he resolved to make a singing career his main goal.

To this end, he began attending auditions during the day, and working as a shelf-stacker at Marks & Spencer and a part-time cleaner in an office block by night.

'I'd decided to take a year out and really give the singing a go,' he recalled later. 'I didn't want to live with the regret that I hadn't tried.' If he didn't

the boy had a real gift.'

But it was not until Danny was 18 that he first realised that his particular talent might be singing. He and his grandparents were on holiday in Tenerife. His grandmother, Patricia, said: 'One of the waiters in the hotel was singing. Danny just got up on stage and started singing *La Bamba* in Spanish. We couldn't believe it.'

Danny had left school at the age of 17, with nine GCSEs. He decided to study for a two-year diploma in nursery nursing and childcare at the City and Islington College in Holloway, north London. But at the same time, he was keen to pursue his singing. He began working as a disc jockey in the evenings, and holding karaoke nights in pubs and clubs.

His former girlfriend, Chloe Price, said: 'Danny always wanted to be a singer. It was his big dream and I knew he would succeed. He used

nothing but hear'say

old, Danny's mum, Tracy, moved to Essex (his dad had left home before Danny was born). Rather than face the upheaval of moving with her, Danny decided to stay with his grandparents, Patricia and Reg, in their council flat.

'Danny doesn't like change,' his grandmother explained later. 'When his mum wanted to get her own place, he didn't want to change schools. Tracy has moved back now and lives only round the corner.'

It was a tough neighbourhood, and some of Danny's schoolfriends would later turn to crime. But that was not a path he was ever likely to follow. He worked hard at school, and his teacher, Ian Robinson, said: 'Danny never got up on stage at school, but his 100-watt smile could light up any screen.'

He also got involved with his local church, and began running a youth club. The Reverend George Bush, of St Anne's Church, in Hoxton, east London, said: 'He's a very genuine, likeable lad. When he organised a disco party I could tell

chapter six
Danny

He might get up on stage in front of thousands of people now, but Danny Foster has never been one for drawing attention to himself. As his new fellow band members have discovered, Danny is reserved, even shy, and during the auditions for *Popstars* he sometimes seemed to lack confidence. But throughout his life, other people have been swift to spot his talent.

Danny was born on May 3 1979, in Shoreditch, east London. When he was 11 years-

Despite her situation, Kym did not give up her quest for success. She appeared on a Channel 4 show called *The Word* as a backing singer for a group called Mother Earth, and even made it into the Top 100 in the charts, with a single called *Day By Day* that she recorded with a house music act called Solar Stone.

But it was her father, David, who first heard about the *Popstars* auditions on a local TV news report. 'My dad was really excited but I knew there were going to be thousands there and the chances were I wasn't going to get anywhere,' said Kym. Her first instinct was not to go. But finally her dad insisted. Eventually, Kym agreed to give it a try.

Fame, however, seemed far away then. Kym separated from David, and life as a single parent was not easy. So while she still feels guilty about leaving her children to be looked after by her parents while she works with the *Popstars* band, Kym knows the alternative is worse. 'I am solely in the *Popstars* band for them. If I thought their lives were becoming miserable because I wasn't there I would give it up immediately.'

The fact that Kym was a mother-of-two was not known until after she had gone through the *Popstars* auditions, because she feared that it would jeopardise her chances of a place in the band. She said later: 'If any single parents are reading this, I'd like to tell them: "Don't give up. If you want to do something with your life then do it."

'And just because you have children it doesn't mean your life ends. In fact, it's just the beginning because you have someone who depends on you.'

nothing but hear'say

a critical condition. 'I'm not deeply religious but I do believe in God, and that night I prayed: "please, please." ' Her father pulled through, and is today in good health again.

The other thing was that Kym and David found out that Kym was expecting a baby. Kym's happiness was tempered a little by her father's state of health. 'Her dad had just had a heart attack and she was worried about him,' said her mum, Pauline. 'But once she realised that we were all behind her she was fine.'

Kym gave birth to her son, David – named after her father – in 1995. Two years later, she had a daughter, Emily. But she still pursued her hopes of a singing career.

Kym's close friend, Kath Hughes, who used to sing with her, said: 'She was performing at the odd club, but it would only be £50 a time, maybe once or twice a week. And on Saturdays she went to Blackpool to teach kids singing for £10. That's why seeing her enjoying her fame is so good.'

is going to make it.'"

But for a while in her teens, Kym experienced problems with her weight. 'When she was 16, she weighed less than seven stone,' her mum remembered. 'She was terribly thin and I was really concerned about her.' Pauline believes that it was meeting her boyfriend, a local builder called David Cunliffe, that saved Kym. 'He was good for her. He's a very funny man and he made her happy. Once she fell in love she was fine and her weight went back to normal.' But Kym would be given a sharp reminder of her teenage illness shortly after joining the *Popstars* band.

At the age of 18, Kym had two life-changing experiences. One of these was her father's heart attack, which left him seriously ill for a while. As soon as she heard the news, Kym rushed to the hospital where her mum was already waiting, to be told that her dad was in

auditions came when, aged 15, she narrowly failed to win a national talent competition. She came third – an achievement in itself – and won a £100 prize at the show in Liverpool. But according to DJ Joe Curran, who hosted the contest, that came as precious little consolation at the time. 'She was so disappointed,' he said. 'She'd done brilliantly to get there, but she really wanted to win.'

Her determination was also noticed by photographer Ray Lewis, when he met the then 16-year-old on a photo shoot at his Merseyside studio. Kym wanted cover photographs for an early recording, and Ray recalled: 'It doesn't surprise me one bit that she's become a star. Even at 16 she was a very determined young lady.

'She knew what she wanted and she was going to make sure she got it. She was very, very positive and a real natural in front of the camera. And she had this powerful voice. She sang for us during the shoot and we were all amazed. I remember my assistant Maureen saying: "This girl

proudly kept the reference written for her by the show's co-presenters, Richard Madeley and Judy Finnigan.

At the same time, Kym was also chosen to appear in a music festival in Poland. 'It was an Eastern Bloc version of the Eurovision song contest,' said her dad. 'In the run-up to the competition, the video for One Kiss was apparently shown all the time on Polish television, so when she arrived in Poland she was already famous. She got off the plane and there were cameras and people waiting. She thought there must be someone famous coming, but it was all for her. They were screaming for her.'

Kym was by far the youngest performer in what was really an adult competition. But she came second. 'She was delighted and really thought that things would start to happen for her,' said Pauline. 'But then it all just seemed to peter out.'

An early taste of the tensions that Kym would later experience during the Popstars

teacher there, Annette Thomson, can remember her. 'She was always well behaved and never mischievous. Kym was one of those pupils who always had it in her to make it big; she had that determination to succeed.' Her elder brother, Jonathan, (Kym is the youngest of four) recalled: 'I would wait outside for her and crease up with laughter at all the weird noises she made. Kym would come out and do hilarious impersonations of the singing teacher. She was always messing around.'

While still at Elliot Clarke stage school, Kym was then spotted by a local record company. She stayed with them for seven years, working as a backing singer for bands including Curiosity Killed The Cat and Black Box. At other times, she was simply the office 'gofer'. But it gave her an invaluable insight into the music world, and while there she also recorded her first single.

It was called *One Kiss*, and as a result of it she appeared on television for the first time on ITV's daytime show, *This Morning*. Afterwards Kym

'Goodness knows how she knew the words. She never faltered and was completely in tune. When the place broke into thunderous applause our little girl was in her element. We were so proud of her and a little shocked that such a powerful voice could come from a ten-year-old.'

Kym was hooked, and started appearing at the club every Sunday. She was obviously talented. But it made her enemies at school. 'I was always doing a show or something so I never hung around the discos, never had a boyfriend,' she said. 'I was always being called a square. But it didn't do me any harm in the end.'

Soon afterwards she joined a children's dance troupe in Liverpool called the Starlight Roadshow. Her first break came when she went for an audition for a professional production of the musical, *Annie*, at the Empire Theatre, Liverpool, and got the part of Kate. One of her co-stars was the actor Bill Maynard.

At the age of 14, she got a place at the Elliot Clarke stage school, also in Liverpool. Her head